The Cottage Cheese Prepared Many Ways

A Cookbook That Tells All!

BY: Ivy Hope

Copyright © 2021 by Ivy Hope

IVY HOPE
COOKBOOK

Copyright/License Page

Please don't reproduce this book. It means you are not allowed to make any type of copy (print or electronic), sell, publish, disseminate or distribute. Only people who have written permission from the author are allowed to do so.

This book is written by the author taking all precautions that the content is true and helpful. However, the reader needs to be careful about his/her action. If anything happens due to the reader's actions the author won't be taken as responsible.

Table of Contents

Introduction 5

   Cottage ideal for the lunchbox 7

   Cake and cottage cheese together 9

   Cottage cheese stuffed enchiladas 11

   Cottage cheese, fruits and granola in a cup 13

   Yummy cottage cheese, ham and cucumber sandwich 15

   Fun and convenient egg muffins with cottage cheese 17

   Fried cottage cheese patties 19

   Special Mac and cheese made with cottage cheese 21

   Fresh tomatoes salad made with love and cottage cheese 23

   Making a yummy bread with nuts and cottage cheese 25

   Cottage cheese and zucchinis fried curds 27

   Vegetables and cottage cheese pie 30

   Simple breakfast: fresh fruits and cottage cheese 32

   A snack for everyone: toasts, cottage cheese and cinnamon 34

   Gourmet cottage cheese stuffed celery 36

Cottage cheese creative appetizers 38

Cottage cheese everyday dip or spread 40

The perfect pizza made with cottage cheese 42

Nachos made with cottage cheese and surprises 44

Stuffed sweet peppers with cottage cheese and herbs 46

Let's prepare potato salad with cottage cheese this time 48

Devil's eggs made with some cottage cheese 50

Dijon and cottage cheese chicken in sauce 52

Small fun stuffed tortillas 55

Get ready for spectacular brownies made with cottage cheese 57

Conclusion 59

About the Author 61

Author's Afterthoughts 62

Introduction

We know you are always curious to learn more about the main ingredients you decide to use in all your recipes. This cookbook is aiming to respect these expectations. In this section, we will talk about many ways to use cottage cheese in the recipe, its history, and other facts. Let's dive right in!

Let us start with its origin. It is quite interesting. Let us talk about the origin of cheese. It appears that it first 5000 years before Christ, in the Middle East area. Apparently, they were spotted in the carvings of some temples, and were made with a combination of milk and salty sour mixture. Although that is very primitive, it changed the destiny of the cheese as we know it today.

In the 19th century, many things happened, including the fact that some farmers started making what they called at that time "Dutch cheese". But what they used is milk that was already bad but that they did not want to waste at the time. It is only in the mid-19th century that the name cottage cheese was given to the lumpy cheese and the processes were refined. Also, we must point out that cottage cheese was used as a great cheap alternative to meat during WW's. Fast-forwarding to the 1970's, more than 1 billion dollars of cottage cheese was sold in the united states alone. In 2016, so recently, the Wall street journal mentioned that cottage cheese could make another big entrance, as the Greek yogurt did a few years ago. This was cottage cheese evolution in a nutshell.

What about its nutritional content? In 100 grams or about ½ cup, you will get about 80 calories. You will also get on average 3 grams of carbs, 4 grams of fat, 11 grams of proteins. Additionally, you can count on the cottage cheese to give you the following vitamins and minerals: calcium, iron, magnesium, potassium, phosphorous, zinc, and sodium.

Finally, let us quickly review the pros and cons of eating cottage cheese. First, cottage cheese is rather inexpensive. Second, it is convenient, easy to mix and prepare in many different ways. Finally, it provides a lot of different nutrients, including proteins. The cons are including the lack of variety. Unlike yogurt where you have many flavors and brands to choose from, the choices in cottage cheese are rather limited. Cottage cheese does not give you any intake of fiber and also contains quite a bit of sodium, so be careful about these aspects.

Cottage ideal for the lunchbox

If you don't know what to pack for your husband or your kid's lunchbox, cottage cheese and veggies or fruits are the best answer. If you pack fruits, you can add some nuts, a pinch of cinnamon, or honey. On the other hand, if you pack with veggies, you can add some Italian herbs or a little dried ranch dressing. Either way, do not forget to pack it with an ice pack to keep it nice and cool.

Serving Size: 1

Cooking Time: 10- Minutes

Ingredients:

- 1 cup cottage cheese
- Your choice of veggies: baby carrots, celery, broccoli florets, grape tomatoes
- Your choice of fruits: strawberries, pears, peaches, apples
- Added spices or herbs as you wish

Instructions:

1) Pack the items of your choice in a divided container.

2) Make sure you refrigerate until inserted in the lunchbox.

Cake and cottage cheese together

Think of cottage cheese in a cake as similar to sour cream. Many recipes require some sour cream, it replaces milk and makes the cake so moist. This will be similar, however, the cottage cheese also adds a salty taste, so avoid adding a pinch of salt like most cake recipes suggest here in this particular case.

Serving Size: 6-8

Cooking Time: 60 minutes

Ingredients:

- 2 cups all-purpose flour
- 1 medium eggs
- ½ tsp. baking powder
- 1 cup cottage cheese
- ½ cup melted coconut oil
- ¾ cup white sugar
- 1 tsp. vanilla
- 2 tbsp. Water
- ½ tsp. baking soda
- Pinch cinnamon

Instructions:

1) Preheat the oven to 350 degrees F.

2) Grease a cake dish and set aside.

3) In a large mixing bowl, combine the dried ingredients.

4) In a second bowl, mix the wet ingredients.

5) Combine in the largest bowl the two mixtures.

6) Pour the cake batter into the dish and bake for 45 minutes.

7) Make sure it is cooled all the way and cut pieces for everyone.

Cottage cheese stuffed enchiladas

This recipe will make everyone happy. It is for sure delicious, but for those watching their weight, it is also healthy and lower calories than an original enchiladas recipe. There will be no high-fat cheese, but just some cottage cheese and other yummy ingredients.

Serving Size: 4

Cooking Time: 50 Minutes

Ingredients:

- 8 small soft tortillas
- 2 cups cottage cheese
- 2 cups enchilada sauce
- 1 Tbsp. Chili powder
- ½ cup salsa
- Minced fresh cilantro
- 1 tbsp. Minced garlic
- 1 tbsp. Lemon juice
- Some olive oil

Instructions:

1) Preheat the oven to 325-degrees F.

2) Grease a rectangle baking dish and set aside.

3) In a small pan, heat the oil and sauté the garlic, lemon juice and cilantro for 4-5 minutes.

4) In a mixing bowl, combine the cottage cheese, salsa, cooked veggies and chili powder.

5) Fill your tortillas with the mixture and roll them tightly.

6) Place them in the baking dish and add the enchilada sauce on top.

7) Bake in the oven for 30 minutes.

Cottage cheese, fruits and granola in a cup

This can make a nice breakfast or a perfect snack for your little ones or big ones within your family. I like to make this easy recipe the best with berries: strawberries, raspberries, blueberries, or even blackberries. You pick your favorite and go for it!

Serving Size: 2

Cooking Time: 10 Minutes

Ingredients:

- 1 ½ cups fresh raspberries
- 1 cup cottage cheese
- ½ cup favorite granolas cereals

Instructions:

1) Get two dessert cups out.

2) Wash and rinse carefully your fresh raspberries. Drain them well.

3) Place an equal amount of granola in each cup.

4) Divide the cottage cheese next.

5) Finally, add the fresh fruits on top.

6) If you are making this a dessert, feel free to add whipped cream on top.

Yummy cottage cheese, ham and cucumber sandwich

This sandwich is quite unusual. I bet you never tasted a sandwich with cottage cheese in it? But you may have had some toast with cottage cheese for breakfast. So, this is not much different. What is mandatory here to remember is that you need to toast the bread to avoid getting mushy.

Serving Size: 2

Cooking Time: 15 Minutes

Ingredients:

- 4 thick slices of wheat bread
- 4 slices of smoked ham
- ¼ cup cottage cheese
- Salt, black pepper
- ¼ sliced cucumber
- Mayonnaise

Instructions:

1) As mentioned before, toast your bread and spread some mayonnaise.

2) In a bowl, combine cottage cheese and salt and pepper.

3) Assemble the sandwich with meat, cottage cheese and cucumber. If you wish, you can add a little salt directly to the cucumbers.

Fun and convenient egg muffins with cottage cheese

Instead of making a quiche, let's make egg muffins. Sure, you can opt for a quiche, but these are crustless and slightly healthier and so practical to pack for lunch, breakfast, or pre-workout snack.

Serving Size: 8

Cooking Time: 50 Minutes

Ingredients:

- 8 large eggs
- ½ tsp onion powder
- 1 cup cottage cheese
- ½ tsp garlic powder
- ¼ diced red bell pepper
- ½ small, sliced zucchini
- ½ cup Swiss cheese
- Salt, black pepper
- Pinch ground cumin
- Some unsalted butter

Instructions:

1) Preheat the oven to 375 degrees.

2) Grease an 8 holes muffin pan, set aside.

3) In a large bowl, combine the eggs, cottage cheese and spices.

4) In a medium pan, sauté for 5 minutes the zucchini and bell pepper.

5) Add to the mixture the veggies and the Swiss cheese. Combine once more.

6) Divide the mixture into 8 and fill the muffin pan.

7) Bake in the oven for 40 minutes.

8) Refrigerate any leftovers and eat on the go anytime!

Fried cottage cheese patties

This is different. You may be used to fried Parmesan square, fried cheese curds, or even fried Feta. However, because cottage cheese is so milky, it is not often used to make fried cheese patties. So, we will need to mix it with something else.

Serving Size: 4

Cooking Time: 40 Minutes

Ingredients:

- 2 cups cottage cheese
- 2 cups panko breadcrumbs
- 1 large egg
- 4 tbsp. All-purpose flour
- ½ tsp. baking powder
- ½ tsp. onion powder
- ½ tsp garlic powder
- Pinch salt and black pepper
- Frying oil

Instructions:

1) In a large mixing bowl, combine the cottage cheese, the spices and the egg.

2) Add gradually the flour, keep stirring to make sure it starts getting thicker and less milky.

3) Add half of the breadcrumbs and start forming the patties.

4) Place the rest of the breadcrumbs in a plate and start coating the patties with breadcrumbs, all around.

5) Heat the oil in a large pan high enough to be frying the patties.

6) Add them all at the same time in the oil and cook for 10 minutes on each side.

7) Flip them carefully when it's time, so they don't start crumbled.

Special Mac and cheese made with cottage cheese

There are many types of cheeses used to make a baked macaroni and cheese. I have made it with mozzarella before, cheddar cheese, parmesan cheese, and even goat cheese. Making this dish with cottage cheese is a nice alternative, but adding another cheese makes it even more delicious.

Serving Size: 4-6

Cooking Time: 60 Minutes

Ingredients:

- 2 cups cottage cheese
- 1 ½ cups shredded Parmesan cheese
- 1 tsp. nutmeg
- 1 cup whole milk
- 2 tbsp. Butter
- 2 Tbsp. All-purpose flour
- 1 box uncooked macaroni elbow pasta
- Salt, black pepper
- ½ tsp. yellow mustard
- 1 cup Italian breadcrumbs

Instructions:

1) Preheat the oven 400 degrees f.

2) Grease a large baking dish and set aside.

3) In a large saucepan, heat water with salt and cook the pasta.

4) While it's cooking, take a second pot, medium size and heat the butter and the flour together on low. Stir to make a roux.

5) Add gradually the milk and the nutmeg.

6) Bring to boil and keep stirring so the milk gets thicker. Remove from the heat.

7) In a large mixing bowl, combine the cottage cheese, mustard, Parmesan cheese, salt, black pepper and add the milk mixture.

8) Once the pasta is cooked, drain, and add to the mixture. Dum it all in the baking dish.

9) Add the breadcrumbs on top and bake for 30 minutes.

Fresh tomatoes salad made with love and cottage cheese

This salad is beautiful because it is colorful. It will showcase some red from the tomatoes, some black from the olives, white from the cottage cheese and cucumber and green onions for more colors. Add some spices and there it is!

Serving Size: 4

Cooking Time: 45 Minutes

Ingredients:

- 1 large, sliced cucumber
- 2 cups grape tomatoes
- 2 cups cottage cheese
- ¼ cup sliced black olives
- 1 medium mixed green onion
- 1 Tbsp. Fresh minced parsley
- 3 Tbsp. Italian dressing
- Black pepper, salt

Instructions:

1) In a large mixing bowl, combine the dressing, spices, onions and parsley.

2) Add the tomatoes and cucumbers, olives and combine.

3) Add the cottage cheese last or even right before you are ready to serve it.

4) Taste the salad to make sure the seasoning is on point.

5) Adjust the seasonings as needed and divide them equally into bowls.

Making a yummy bread with nuts and cottage cheese

I think you know by now that sour cream can often be substitute one for another. Because cottage cheese is salty, you may want to think to add brown sugar, honey, or even agave sugar. One thing is sure is that you do need to add some sweetener, and we will suggest one in the recipe below.

Serving Size: 4-8

Cooking Time: 60 Minutes

Ingredients:

- 2 cups coconut flour
- 1 cup cottage cheese
- ½ cup all-purpose flour
- 2 medium eggs
- 1 tsp. baking powder
- 1 cup brown sugar
- Pinch cinnamon
- ½ tsp. Baking soda
- 3 tbsp. Melted coconut oil

Instructions:

1) Preheat the oven to 350 degrees F.

2) Grease a bread pan and set aside.

3) In a first medium mixing bowl, combine the dry ingredients: flours, sugar, cinnamon, baking powder and baking soda.

4) In a second bowl, combine the eggs, coconut oil, cottage cheese.

5) Add the wet mixture to the dried one and combine again.

6) Dump into the baking dish and bake for 45 to 50 minutes or until done.

Cottage cheese and zucchinis fried curds

We are going to suggest frying cottage cheese once again! We know why! Because we think it's delicious. These curds can be served as appetizers, you just have to make them at the last minute because they need to be served hot and they will melt in your guests' mouths.

Serving Size: 4-6

Cooking Time: 30 Minutes

Ingredients:

- 1 large diced zucchini
- 2 tbsp. Diced sweet onions
- ½ tbsp. Minced garlic
- 2 large eggs
- 1 ½ cups all-purpose flour
- 1 tsp. Baking powder
- 1 ½ cups cottage cheese
- Pinch cumin
- Salt, black pepper
- Unsalted butter

Instructions:

1) In a medium pan, heat some butter and sauté the zucchinis, garlic and onions together for 5minutes.

2) In a large mixing bowl, combine the eggs, cottage cheese.

3) Add the cooked veggies and all spices. Combine again.

4) Gradually add the flour and then the baking powder.

5) By then, you should be able to form easily some little balls.

6) Get the oil heated in a large frying pan.

7) If you think the mixture needs more moisture, add a little cottage cheese or if it needs more flour, do so as well.

8) Fry the balls or curds in the hot oil for about 15 minutes. Rotate them quite often so they are goldening all the way around.

9) Serve with ranch dressing or your favorite dipping sauce, such as horseradish sauce or even sweet and sour sauce.

Vegetables and cottage cheese pie

This is similar to a quiche. And this can be an awesome vegetarian complete meal or served as a side with some baked fish. Let's try it today!

Serving Size: 4

Cooking Time: 60 Minutes+

Ingredients:

- 2 pie crusts (1 deep and one for the top)
- 2 larger sliced fresh tomatoes
- ½ cup diced yellow onion
- 5 large eggs
- ½ cup kernel corn
- 1 tbsp. Minced garlic
- 1/2 cup cottage cheese
- 2 cups shredded Sharp Cheddar
- Salt, black pepper
- Unsalted butter

Instructions:

1) Preheat the oven to 375 degrees F.

2) Gather all ingredients. Heat butter in a medium pan and add the onion and garlic, sauté 5 minutes.

3) In a large bowl, combine the eggs, cottage cheese, cheddar cheese, salt, pepper and cooked veggies.

4) Dump that mixture into the deep pie crust.

5) Lay the sliced tomatoes on top and season with black pepper before covering the pie with the top pie crust.

6) Brush a little butter on the crust and place in the oven for 50 minutes or until the crust is golden.

Simple breakfast: fresh fruits and cottage cheese

This simple breakfast can be served any day of the week with fresh fruits. I sometimes combine some canned fruits, such as peaches and pears with some fresh apples or kiwis, for example. You can add a little light syrup from the canned fruits if you like. Also, if you want the extra fiber and proteins, please take our lead and add some chia seeds as we suggest here.

Serving Size: 4

Cooking Time: 15 Minutes

Ingredients:

- 2 cups cottage cheese
- 3 medium size kiwis
- 2 large, peeled oranges
- 1 large, sliced apple
- Little lemon juice
- 1 Tbsp. Chia seeds
- Pinch cinnamon

Instructions:

1) Get all ingredients out.

2) Also, get 4 small bowls out.

3) Prepare all the fruits and once you sliced the apple, add a little lemon juice, so it does not turn brownish.

4) Divide the cottage cheese into 4 bowls. Add the prepared fruits equally into each bowl.

5) Sprinkle some chia seeds and some cinnamon on top of the fruits. Serve to your family with love!

A snack for everyone: toasts, cottage cheese and cinnamon

If you can use cinnamon sticks and ground them fresh, it could be one of the best cinnamon toasts you even made. If you cannot, using ground cinnamon is also fine. Make sure your cottage cheese is the large curds one. Also butter up your bread!

Serving Size: 2

Cooking Time: 20 Minutes

Ingredients:

- 1 small baguette
- 1 cinnamon stick, grinded freshly or 1 tsp. of ground cinnamon
- 1 cup large curd cottage cheese
- 2 tsp. Unsalted butter

Instructions:

1) Preheat the oven to 425 degrees.

2) Grease a small baking sheet.

3) Cut the baguette into 4 lengthwise slices.

4) Spread butter on them and toast them in the oven for 10 minutes.

5) Mix the cottage cheese with cinnamon while the bread toasting.

6) Right away when they are out, spread the cottage cheese on each slice.

7) Eat with cup of coffee.

8) I often also drizzle a little honey on the toasts, and it is quite good.

Gourmet cottage cheese stuffed celery

Eating celery maybe not so interesting to many. It is a very plain vegetable but extremely high in fiber. So, my mom used to serve it with creamy peanut butter or spread of some cream cheese on it. In this recipe, we suggest a cottage cheese mixture to put on the celery.

Serving Size: 4

Cooking Time: 20 Minutes

Ingredients:

- 2 cups of cottage cheese
- 1 Tbsp. Minced chives
- 1 Tbsp. hot sauce
- Some smoked paprika
- 6 stalks of celery, cut into 3 pieces

Instructions:

1) Wash and cut into 3 pieces the celery.

2) Place them on a serving plate or in a large container is you are making them ahead.

3) In a mixing bowl, combine the cheese, hot sauce. Spread onto each celery stick.

4) Sprinkle some smoked paprika on each of them.

Cottage cheese creative appetizers

I think when it is time to make appetizers, there are a few things to remember. It should be about colors and variety. If you are hosting a party, you want to have some proteins, some veggies, and perhaps some fine herbs and the right seasonings. Also, the crackers or bread you will be using should be diversified. Please use your imagination here to create the bites but also choose so many variety of ingredients to combine!

Serving Size: 10-12

Cooking Time: 20-25 Minutes

Ingredients:

- Multigrain crackers
- Rye crackers
- 1 ½ cups cottage cheese
- 1 package of cream cheese, plain, room temperature
- 1 Tbsp. Minced parsley
- Some diced smoked salmon
- Some diced Black Forest ham
- ½ cup diced marinated beets
- Some diced pickles
- Black pepper

Instructions:

1) Combine cottage cheese, cream cheese and the cracked pepper in a medium bowl.

2) Get all the other ingredients out and line them up.

3) On a serving plate, lay down the crackers, mixing both kinds on the plate.

4) Spread a generous portion of the cheese on each cracker.

5) On half of them, add some smoked salmon and beets. On the other half, add some ham and pickles.

6) Add some minced parsley on top of the crackers as you wish.

7) Refrigerate if you are not ready to serve right away.

Cottage cheese everyday dip or spread

This dip can replace any sour cream or mayonnaise dip you usually make for your family. I love the nutty taste we add and certainly savory overall for everyone to enjoy. If you can find some fresh herbs to add, you may even enjoy it more. You can easily warm up this dip and serve it warm for everyone to enjoy if you prefer.

Serving Size: 8-10

Cooking Time: 50 Minutes

Ingredients:

- 2 cups cottage cheese
- ½ cup sour cream
- ½ cup chopped walnut
- ¼ cup roasted sunflowers
- ½ tbsp. Minced fresh chives
- ½ tsp. onion powder
- Salt, black pepper

Instructions:

1) Use a large mixing bowl ad place the cottage cheese, sour cream and seasonings.

2) Combine well with a wooden spoon and add the herbs and the nuts.

3) Stir again and taste, adjust seasonings as needed. You are all done!

The perfect pizza made with cottage cheese

I have made pizza with just about all kinds of cheeses. I think most pizzas do use some shredded Mozzarella as a very well-known melting cheese. Here, we will use one of the cheeses that melt the less, but we will pair it with another one to help its use. In this recipe, we will also add some sundried tomatoes for a change. Don't forget that when you choose the pie crust you like, you can go with thin or thick.

Serving Size: 3-4

Cooking Time: 40 Minutes

Ingredients:

- 1 cup fresh baby spinach
- 2/3 cup cottage cheese
- ½ cup shredded Parmesan cheese
- ¼ cup diced sundried tomatoes
- ¼ cup sliced red onion
- 1/2 Tbsp. Minced garlic
- ½ tsp. dried Italian herbs
- Little olive oil
- Black pepper
- 1 large pie crust

Instructions:

1) Preheat oven to 400 degrees F.

2) Grease a pizza pan and set aside.

3) In a bowl, combine the cottage cheese, garlic and Parmesan cheese.

4) Brush some olive oil on the crust and sprinkle dried herbs and black pepper.

5) Next, spread the mixture of cheese evenly.

6) Top it off with sundried tomatoes, onions and baby spinach

7) Bake the pizza in the oven for 25-30 minutes.

8) Serve with some seasoned oil if you like.

Nachos made with cottage cheese and surprises

This may be a first as well! We all know nachos can or are usually served with melted Cheddar cheese or queso sauce. Here, we will make the cottage cheese topping taste quite incredible, so you will forget it is not the typical cheese you find on nachos. Feel free to add your favorite toppings.

Serving Size: 4

Cooking Time: 50 Minutes

Ingredients:

- 1 bag of tortillas chips
- 2 cups cottage cheese
- ½ cup diced green chili peppers
- Few handfuls of diced black olives
- ½ cup diced fresh tomatoes
- 1 minced green onion
- 2 cups grilled chicken breasts
- 1 tsp. chili powder

Instructions:

1) Preheat the oven to 325 degrees F.

2) Grease a large baking dish and set aside.

3) In a medium mixing bowl, combine the cottage cheese, green chili peppers, chili powder and green onion.

4) Place the tortilla chips on the bottom of the dish.

5) Add the cottage cheese mixture next. Then the chicken, olives and tomatoes.

6) Place in the oven for about 20 minutes.

7) Serve with salsa and sour cream.

Stuffed sweet peppers with cottage cheese and herbs

I enjoy buying a full bag of sweet peppers when they are in season or on sale. I enjoy making different recipes with them or simply use them in salads or stir fry. They are smaller than the regular bell peppers and sweeter. What I really love about them is that they come in fabulous colors: yellow, orange, and red. So, let's fill them up with a tasty mixture and make it special.

Serving Size: 4-6

Cooking Time: 45 minutes

Ingredients:

- 8-10 small, sweet peppers, different colors
- 1 cup cottage cheese
- 1 package cream cheese with garlic and herbs, room temperature
- 1 Tbsp. Minced fresh parsley
- 1 tbsp. Minced fresh chives
- Salt, black pepper
- Smoked paprika
- Olive oil

Instructions:

1) Preheat the oven to 400 degrees F.

2) Grease a baking sheet and set aside.

3) Wash and cut all the sweet peppers in halves. Remove all the seeds from the peppers.

4) In a large mixing bowl, combine the cheeses, chives, parsley, and salt and pepper.

5) Stuff each pepper with the mixture and finish with a pinch of smoked paprika. Also, brush some olive oil on the outside of the peppers.

6) Bake the peppers for about 30-35 minutes and serve as appetizers or as a side with grilled meats, for example.

Let's prepare potato salad with cottage cheese this time

I think we all have had the main version of potato salads by now. I love the one that my mom used to make with red-skinned potatoes and diced pickles. I also had the version with hardboiled eggs in it. Any potato salad does have a couple of things in common which are potatoes and some type of sauce or vinaigrette.

Serving Size: 4-6

Cooking Time: 50 Minutes

Ingredients:

- 2 large peeled white potatoes
- 2 large red skinned potatoes (with skin on)
- Handful diced yellow banana peppers
- Handful of green pepper stuffed olives
- Salt, black pepper
- ½ tsp. celery seeds
- ½ tsp. ground cumin
- 2 diced celery stalks
- 1 ½ cups cottage cheese
- ¼ cup mayonnaise

Instructions:

1) Boil water in a large saucepan and cook the potatoes for about 12-14 minutes or they are slightly soft but not mushy.

2) Drain them well and let them cool down.

3) In a large mixing bowl, combine the mayonnaise, cottage cheese and all seasonings.

4) Add the diced potatoes and combine well.

5) Add also the olives, celery and banana peppers.

6) Combine again and place in containers and in the fridge so it's ready to be served anytime!

Devil's eggs made with some cottage cheese

Oh, I love this recipe! These muffins are packed with flavors and surprises! Now, for the sweet element, we choose peaches. We guarantee that you will like them and enjoy sharing them with your neighbors and friends to see what their reaction will be when they bite into these clashing flavors.

Serving Size: 6-8

Cooking Time: 50 Minutes

Ingredients:

- 12 large eggs
- 1 cup cottage cheese
- ½ cup mayonnaise
- 2 Tbsp. Sweet relish
- 1 tsp. yellow mustard
- Salt, black pepper
- Cayenne pepper

Instructions:

1) Boil water in a large pot and add the 12 eggs. Turn off the heat and keep the pot on the same burner. Put your timer for 20 minutes, that should be enough for them to be done.

2) Once the timer goes off, Rinse the eggs under cold water and immediately remove the shell easily.

3) Set the eggs aside until they cool down.

4) Meanwhile, prepare the filling.

5) Combine in a large bowl, the cottage cheese, mayonnaise, relish, mustard, salt and pepper.

6) Cut the eggs lengthwise and remove the yellow center and add to the mixture.

7) Use a fork to mix it all together.

8) Taste the mixture to check the seasonings and fill each white halved egg

9) Place on your serving plate or in the refrigerator for later.

Dijon and cottage cheese chicken in sauce

I think it is important to make sure that your chicken stays moist. Sometimes you choose to marinate it, sometimes you choose to serve it in a sauce. Today the sauce will be made with cottage cheese and cream and so much more. Stay tuned and stay hungry because this is going to be delicious!

Serving Size: 4

Cooking Time: 45 Minutes

Ingredients:

- 4 large chicken breasts, skinless, boneless
- 1 Tbsp. Dijon mustard
- 1 cup heavy cream
- 1 cup cottage
- 8 slices thick bacon
- 2 cups fresh button mushrooms
- 1 tbsp. Minced garlic
- Unsalted butter
- Salt, black pepper
- Pinch nutmeg
- Little all-purpose flour

Instructions:

1) Preheat the oven to 375 degrees F.

2) Grease a large baking dish and set aside.

3) In a large pan, cook the bacon for 12-15 minutes, flipping it occasionally. When done, leave the grease in the pan and set bacon aside for now.

4) Season with salt and pepper the chicken breasts and sear in the pan in bacon grease for about 3-4 minutes on each side.

5) Meanwhile, in a different pan, heat some butter and start cooking the minced garlic with fresh mushrooms.

6) Once the chicken is cooked and the veggies as well. Start on your third component.

7) Get a medium saucepan and heat some butter and add a little flour on medium heat.

8) Stir constantly to make a roux. Add the cream, Dijon mustard and cottage cheese and then bring to boil.

9) Continue to stir constantly, and make sure it does not stick.

10) Once you see the sauce has thickened, reduce the heat and add a title nutmeg. Stir again and then add the cooked crumbled bacon.

11) Place the chicken on the baking dish and then add the cooked mushrooms and garlic, then top it off with the sauce.

12) Place in the oven for 40 minutes and serve with a side of steamed green beans.

Small fun stuffed tortillas

I love wraps and it is such a fun and simple sandwich to make any day of the week. You can buy them in different flavors and colors, maybe spinach or sundried tomatoes or even garlic and herbs. We choose chicken for this recipe but remember that you can also make them with tuna or even smoked sliced ham.

Serving Size: 4

Cooking Time: 20 minutes

Ingredients:

- 4 mediums size tortilla breads (your choice of flavors and colors)
- 1 cup baby spinach leaves
- 1 cup cottage cheese
- 2 tbsp. Mayonnaise
- 2 cans of chicken breasts flakes
- 1 tbsp. Dried Italian herbs
- Salt, black pepper

Instructions:

1) Let us start by making the filling. In a medium mixing bowl, combine the mayonnaise, cottage cheese, dried herbs, salt, black pepper. Combine well.

2) Add the well-drained chicken from the can next. Combine with a fork.

3) Place your breads flat on the plates and spread a generous portion of the mixture and add some spinach leaves as well. Roll up these wraps and cut them in halves.

Get ready for spectacular brownies made with cottage cheese

These little bites are a great mixture of smoked, salty, and sweet. I don't know if it can get any better. They are fabulous to look at, so it is such a great, you do need to make them at your next party or family gathering. Also, they are so easy to make! Let's try it!

Serving Size: 4

Cooking Time: 45 Minutes

Ingredients:

- 2 cups all-purpose flour
- 3 tbsp. Unsalted butter
- ½ tsp. baking soda
- 1 large egg
- 2/3 cup brown sugar
- ¾ cup cottage cheese
- 1 Tbsp. Cocoa powder
- ½ cup chocolate chips
- ½ tsp. baking powder
- Pinch salt

Instructions:

1) Preheat the oven to 350 degrees F.

2) Grease a square baking dish and set aside.

3) In a large mixing bowl, combine the dry ingredients: flour, sugar, baking powder, cocoa powder, baking soda and salt.

4) In a second bowl, combine the wet ingredients: egg, butter, cottage cheese and stir well.

5) Dump the wet ingredients into the dried ones and also add the chocolate chips.

6) Combine again all together and dump the cholate mixture into your baking dish.

7) Bake in the oven for 40 minutes.

8) Cut into squares when they cooled down and enjoy one with a cold glass of milk.

Conclusion

In this last section, we will play devil's advocate and compare some cheeses to our start of the day, the cottage cheese.

First, let us start with the ricotta cheese. They seem rather similar in texture, so are they interchangeable? Do they taste the same? Are they comparable nutritionally wise? So happy to have taken this with you!

Let us talk about some differences first. The Ricotta cheese is smoother. While the cottage cheese includes some lumps no matter what percentage of fat you choose. The Ricotta cheese is then creamier and slightly sweeter in taste. We can substitute the ricotta for cottage or vice-versa in many recipes. For example, lasagna, quiches, egg muffins, or omelets. You can also interchange the cottage cheese for ricotta in dips. In these cases, you can substitute 1 for 1 (1 cup for 1 cup for example).

What about the nutritional aspect? Apparently, cottage cheese is overall healthier than ricotta cheese. It has lower fat content while providing you some calcium and other beneficial health aspects. However, the Ricotta cheese offers less sodium, so please choose what is best for you and your specific diet.

Another cheese that is wildly used and that we will gladly compare to the cottage cheese is cream cheese. As you can visually tell, they are quite different! Cottage cheese is lumpy or chunky, while cream cheese, as its name says, is creamier.

Cottage cheese is made by curdling the milk, meaning an enzyme or acid is added allowed the milk to turn, then the cheese is drained, leaving the cottage cheese as we know it. In the case of cream cheese, the milk and cream are mixed until a certain thickness is reached, resulting in the creamy cheese we all know so well.

Let's talk about nutritional information for a minute. If we compare a cup of cottage cheese versus the same cream cheese, you will soon find out how much more calories the cream cheese provides. For example, fat wise, a low-fat cup of cottage cheese will give you in general about 160 calories. If you consume the same amount of cream cheese, you will ingest about calories 220 calories.

We briefly described some of the cheese options you have above. Please always educate yourself according to your primary care physician's advice and your own taste.

Enjoy the cottage cheese for what it brings you, including its unique flavor!

About the Author

Ivy's mission is to share her recipes with the world. Even though she is not a professional cook she has always had that flair toward cooking. Her hands create magic. She can make even the simplest recipe tastes superb. Everyone who has tried her food has astounding their compliments was what made her think about writing recipes.

She wanted everyone to have a taste of her creations aside from close family and friends. So, deciding to write recipes was her winning decision. She isn't interested in popularity, but how many people have her recipes reached and touched people. Each recipe in her cookbooks is special and has a special meaning in her life. This means that each recipe is created with attention and love. Every ingredient carefully picked, every combination tried and tested.

Her mission started on her birthday about 9 years ago, when her guests couldn't stop prizing the food on the table. The next thing she did was organizing an event where chefs from restaurants were tasting her recipes. This event gave her the courage to start spreading her recipes.

She has written many cookbooks and she is still working on more. There is no end in the art of cooking; all you need is inspiration, love, and dedication.

Author's Afterthoughts

THANK YOU

I am thankful for downloading this book and taking the time to read it. I know that you have learned a lot and you had a great time reading it. Writing books is the best way to share the skills I have with your and the best tips too.

I know that there are many books and choosing my book is amazing. I am thankful that you stopped and took time to decide. You made a great decision and I am sure that you enjoyed it.

I will be even happier if you provide honest feedback about my book. Feedbacks helped by growing and they still do. They help me to choose better content and new ideas. So, maybe your feedback can trigger an idea for my next book.

Thank you again

Sincerely

Ivy Hope

Made in the USA
Middletown, DE
27 August 2022